PRINCE HARRY BOOK

The Biography of Prince Harry

University Press

CONTENTS

INTRODUCTION

Prince Harry, 33 years old, stood just below the altar in St George's Chapel at Windsor Castle, looking sheepishly out over the cavernous room, which was presently packed with many of his closest friends, as well as plenty of celebrities, government officials, and--of course--members of the extended Royal Family. Harry had been at Windsor Castle for hours, but he hadn't been waiting as long as some of the guests. The public had started arriving at the castle grounds as early as 8:00 that morning. An event of this magnitude--with over 2,000 members of the public invited to the grounds, around 600 high-profile guests inside the building, a security budget estimated at over 2 million pounds, and hundreds of millions of people tuning in live around the world--would have a lot of moving parts. Nothing would happen quickly; a lot of waiting was involved.

Harry tugged at the hem of his frock coat uniform,

the formal dress uniform of the Blues and Royals (or the Royal Horse Guards and 1st Dragoons), in an effort to calm his nerves. Just that morning, Harry's grandmother, Queen Elizabeth II, had conferred upon him the title of Duke of Sussex, as well as the secondary titles of Earle of Dumbarton and Baron Kilkeel. The full weight of these appointments had already set in. Harry, who grew up in the Royal Family, was not phased by titles or honors. But what he would be doing now was a completely different story. Today, he would take on a new title and role that he felt much less prepared to assume, a title that carried with it far less international and historic prestige but was life-changing, nonetheless. That title, a daunting one for any man, was *husband*.

Today, Harry was getting married.

Finally, just a little after noon, the bride arrived. Meghan Markle, an American actress and blogger, probably best known prior to this for her role in the American law drama Suits, wore an elegant, white wedding dress with a boat neckline that just hinted at slipping off the shoulders, long sleeves and a sweeping train that was just a bit longer than the 16-foot silk veil, an entire dress a garment of the finest silk, designed by Clare Waight Keller of the French luxury fashion house Givenchy. In a bold display of feminist principles, Meghan began her bridal procession without a male escort, accompanied only by a party of junior attendants. Eventually, she was met by the Prince of Wales, who escorted her through the quire of the chapel and led her to the altar, where Harry was eagerly waiting for her.

The gaze of love and admiration that flashed on Harry's blushing face, which was stippled by a well-trimmed red-haired beard, would be captured by photographers and video cameras and shown to the world as an exemplar of husbandly devotion. And, true, Harry was in love. What other emotions visited his heart that day, some perhaps even bittersweet in nature? Did he wish his mother, Princess Diana, had been there? Mixed in with the love and devotion he felt for Meghan then, was there gratitude to her, as well? After all, as we'll see later in this book, she was instrumental in helping Harry escape a negative downward spiral in his life, a dark time that could have led to ugly self-destruction and public scandal. Certainly, he was proud--not of himself or his country--but of Meghan, who would soon become not only his wife but also the Duchess of Sussex, the Countess of Dumbarton, and Baroness Kilkeel. Their love had brought them together, but it couldn't be easy for a girl that had grown up in LA with a love of theater and film to suddenly be thrown into the world of a British Royal.

A Soldier First, A Prince Second

Few in the United States, and other parts of the world that aren't part of the British Commonwealth, know all that much about Harry beyond his marriage to Meghan Markle. Certainly, the astute viewer of news headlines may recall that he was one of the two young men left motherless after the tragic death of Princess Diana. But there was another major aspect of his life before the wedding that consumed much of his adult life--the military. In fact, for reasons that we'll discuss later in this book, one could argue that Harry has been a soldier first and a prince second.

Harry's military training and career shaped much of his life, and we'll see how this may have grown out of his losing his mother at a young age. His life wasn't just shaped by going to war, which he did do, fighting on the front lines in Afghanistan. But, later in his career, his focus turned to the men and women that sacrificed everything for their country on the battlefield, many of whom are considered "lucky" because they came back alive but seriously wounded. Those that sustained life-changing injuries, such as the loss of a limb, would be marked by war for the rest of their days, and Harry was moved to help such ones in a variety of ways, as we'll see later.

To understand Prince Harry, we must understand his military career. On top of that, we must look at the death of his mother through the eyes of a young man already filled with anguish because of his parents' divorce the year before, and not through the lens of a conspiracy theorist that wants to blame Diana's death on anything from a Royal conspiracy to proof of an alien invasion.

In addition to analyzing Harry's life leading up to his marriage to Meghan Markle, we'll look at events that have completely redirected both of their lives after the internationally transmitted wedding day. Harry's transition from soldier to husband to expat living in Southern California is a fascinating one, setting both Harry and Meghan on a new and exciting, if not somewhat scandalous, path.

This book looks at Prince Harry's life from those perspectives. We'll take a detailed look at Harry's childhood and the struggles that planted seeds of trauma that would later grow into thorny vines to haunt him. We'll look at his schooling and military training, at the fight he had to make in order to join in combat in one of the most dangerous regions in the world. And we'll see how he was rescued from the pit of despair by reaching out and helping others and then finally accepting that he needed help himself.

Finally, we'll see how a new Harry emerged from his experiences and the help her received, a Harry that was ready to take his relationship with a beautiful and mature young American woman to the next level. We'll see how this post-metamorphosis Prince Harry was willing to step away from the pressures and prestige of royal life, turning his back on his roots in many ways, to step into a new world and craft a new life for himself and his family.

This is the story of a young man who has endured enormous pressure and tragedy, a young man who allowed himself to be transformed by those experiences, and who stared out at the abyss and was brought back from the brink of insanity.

This is the story of the origin and transformation of Henry Charles Albert David, better known to the world as Prince Harry.

CHAPTER 1

Heritage and Early Life

As a member of the British Royal Family, Prince Harry can trace his ancestry back hundreds of years. Historians differ on when one could start counting the lineage of the British Royal Family—as distinguished from the royal line of the rest of Europe—but King George III may be a good place to start because, unlike his two predecessors (the first two Georges), George III was born in Great Britain (as opposed to Hanover, Germany, where his family was from), he spoke English as his mother tongue, and he lived in Britain his whole life. George III ruled as King over Britain and Ireland as two distinct nations until 1801, when the two kingdoms merged and the United Kingdom was born, a new nation that George III ruled over for almost 20 years until his death in 1820. King George III is considered the longest-lived and longest-reigning King in all of British history.

George III's granddaughter would grow up to be Queen Victoria, the so-called "grandmother of Europe" whose reign of more than 63 years would make her the longest-reigning monarch over Britain up to that time (monarch, as opposed to King, because Victoria was a woman), beating King George III's 59 years and ushering in the Victorian Era. (Of course, Queen Elizabeth II, Harry's grandmother, would break Victoria's record by ruling for nearly 71 years until her death in 2022.)

Elizabeth II had four children with her husband, Philip, Duke of Edinburgh: Charles, Anne, Andrew, and Edward. Charles, born in 1948, would be named Prince of Wales at the age of ten and then King of the UK after Elizabeth's passing in 2022. Ascending to the throne at the age of 73, King Charles II, as he would now be called, is the oldest one to be crowned King in British history.

Lord Mountbatten told Charles that he should choose a suitable, attractive, and sweet-charactered girl for a wife. Charles would find such a girl in the form of Diana Spencer. But their relationship didn't start out as a romantic one. In fact, Diana was the younger sister of one of Charles' previous girlfriends.

Harry's Mother And Father

Prince Charles first met Lady Diana in 1977 while

visiting her older sister. He didn't even consider her as a potential romantic partner at the time, however. In fact, it was generally assumed that he'd end up marrying his cousin, a young woman named Amanda Knatchbull. Amanda was the granddaughter of Lord Mountbatten, the same uncle that had encouraged Charles to sow his wild oats far and wide before getting married. Amanda was only 16 at the time, but both of her parents approved of the idea of her and Charles getting married when the time was right.

Lord Mountbatten tried to arrange for Charles and Amanda to join him on a tour of India in 1980, but those plans fell through. In the end, Lord Mountbatten was assassinated by the Irish Republican Army in 1979. In 1980, Charles proposed to Amanda, but the young woman was now reluctant to join the royal family after her grandfather's death. The relationship ended soon after.

It was in the summer of 1980 that Prince Charles started to take an interest in Diana, who was still a close friend throughout this time. On one occasion, Diana could see that Charles was feeling down, and she did her best to comfort him. As Charles' biographer puts it, it was at that time that "without any apparent surge in feeling, he began to think seriously of her as a potential bride." They started a relationship soon after, Diana accompanying Charles to various trips and events. The media was already taken in with Diana and the courtship, and Charles felt a good deal of pressure to make a decision. Therefore, even though those close to him told him they didn't think he was really in love with Diana, Charles proposed to her in February of 1981. They'd be married in July of that same year.

Diana was a star in the eyes of the media and the British public. This is in part because, while she was born into the British nobility, there was something down-to-earth and worldly about her, which allowed her to connect with the everyday folk of the country and world. She grew up wealthy and was homeschooled for the early part of her education by a personal governess. But, later, she went to boarding schools and private schools, even though she never really excelled academically. She then spent years bouncing from one job to another, teaching music or dance for a while, or working as a nanny. At one point, she aspired to be a teacher, although her grades at school didn't really make that an option. That's when Prince Charles swooped in and proposed. Diana was overwhelmed by the idea of being in the Royal family, but she felt she couldn't refuse.

Shortly after getting married at the age of twenty and becoming the Princess of Wales, Diana and Charles moved into Kensington Palace. They maintained a second residence at Highgrove House near Tetbury. By the end of 1981, Diana was pregnant. Prince William, Harry's older brother, was born in 1982, and Diana suffered from postpartum depression. A few years later, Diana got pregnant a second time.

On September 15, 1984, her second son was born. Henry Charles Albert David was christened at St George's Chapel in Windsor Castle, the same place he'd later get married. Everyone in the family called Henry Charles "Prince Harry," both within the family and in public. The name stuck, and it's the way he's still known today.

After having Harry, Diana recovered from postpartum depression, which allowed her to take an active and personal interest in raising her two boys. She was determined to give the boys a broad range of experiences—as opposed to just growing up in a castle, shielded from the outside world—so she took Harry and his older brother on a great variety of trips. For example, they'd get food from McDonald's like any other young boy in the UK. They went to Disney World, too. But Diana also made sure the boy saw the sadder parts of the world, so they visited places like homeless shelters and AIDS clinics.

As a young boy, Harry also went on numerous international trips with his parents. From a young age, he traveled to Italy and Canada, among other countries. Diana worked hard to give Harry a good childhood, but things were going to get much darker after his tenth birthday.

National Tragedy

Up until 1987, Harry's parents had been able to keep their marital problems mostly hidden from the public. But cracks were starting to show - especially after the tabloids got involved. In 1991, the couple separated, and in 1996, their marriage ended in divorce.

These years were hellish ones for young Harry, seeing his parents avoid one another for months at a time, except for public appearances. It seemed they'd never get back together, and, in the end, they never did. Diana was public and open about her marital problems - and about her struggles with postpartum depression and bulimia. Harry's exposure to these things would come back to haunt him later in life.

Then, on August 31, 1997, Diana died in a high-speed car accident in Paris. The world mourned Diana's passing, and her funeral was one of the most-viewed events in UK television history. Harry and William were staying at Balmoral Castle, a formidable estate house in Scotland. Charles told his sons about Diana's death, news that would throw 12-year-old Harry's life into chaos for years to come. At the funeral, Harry and his brother joined the rest of the Royal Family in walking behind Diana's carriage.

the Royal Family's dime. He could have stayed in exclusive resorts or rubbed shoulders with some of the world's rich and powerful. Instead, he followed the same train of thought that brought him and his brother to AIDS clinics and homeless shelters. He went to Australia and worked as a jackaroo at a cattle station. Working with his hands in extreme heat, Harry rubbed shoulders with the Australian version of cowboys for months. Then he traveled to the small, landlocked kingdom of Lesotho, a tiny nation embedded in South Africa. There, he worked with orphaned children and helped produce a documentary called *The Forgotten Kingdom*.

Returning from his gap year in 2004, he was ready to turn his attention to the career of his choice, and that meant continuing his education in the form of military training.

CHAPTER 3

Military Training

Before Harry's gap year working as an Australian cowboy, Harry had already laid the groundwork for a military career by joining the Combine Cadet Force while studying at Eton. The Combined Cadet Force often referred to simply as the CCF, is a military training program for students sponsored by the UK's ministry of defense, similar to the ROTC and Junior ROTC programs in the US. BCCF generally includes sections for the army, Royal Navy, and Royal Air Force, and the youth organization's stated purpose is to "provide a disciplined organization in a school that pupils may develop powers of leadership by means of training to promote the qualities of responsibility, self-reliance, resourcefulness, endurance, and perseverance." Certainly, such attributes would greatly help a young member of the royal family, even if they had no intention of entering the military proper.

By the time Harry made it to his final year at Eton, he'd made cadet officer and led the CCF annual parade at the Eton tattoo. After returning from his gap year, Harry was ready to begin his official military training at Sandhurst.

Royal Military Academy

If you intend to become an officer in some branch of the British military, you must go to one of three schools. Britannia royal naval college—located on a hill overlooking the port of Dartmouth in Devon, England—and Royal Air Force College Cranwell—which is part of the Royal Air Force base in Cranwell and boasts of being the world's first air Academy, founded in 1919—are your only options if you want a curvier as a commissioned officer in either the Navy or Air Force. Suppose, like Prince Harry, you have your sights set on a career in the British Army. In that case, you'll have to go for initial officer training at Royal Military Academy Sandhurst, a school more often simply referred to as Sandhurst.

Harry's grades when graduating from Eton were instrumental in his being accepted at Sandhurst, and the fact that a member of the royal family, and a member of the combined cadet force at that, isn't automatically granted acceptance into The Academy is a testament to the high standards the school maintains.

The high standards extend to the instructors, as well. Every year, noncommissioned officers from every part of the British Army apply for 60 hotly contested seats. Then, those instructors go through a demanding set of physical and mental assessments, and only 30 are selected in the end. This selection process, which lasts between three and four weeks, is designed to ensure that the quality of instruction is top-notch. No other institution has such a rigorous selection that perspective instructors have to pass in order to be part of the training team. The age-old adage that "those who can't do, teach" is not true in the case of the Royal Military Academy Sandhurst.

Harry entered Sandhurst in may of 2005. As a student there, he wasn't addressed in the customary way of any member of the royal British family as "your Royal Highness." He wasn't even usually called Prince Harry. Instead, he was known as Officer Cadet Wales.

About 200 cadets enter the Academy at the same time. They are each assigned to a platoon within one of two companies, each company numbering about 100 cadets. The Academy and training up to 10 companies at the same time, and each company is given a unique name based on a battle or campaign from the history of the British Army. For example, Harry was assigned to Alamein Company, named after El Alamein, a town in Egypt where two battles were fought during World War Two. The so-called second battle of El Alamein took place at the end of October and the beginning of November in 1942, an intense series of desert conflicts between the British Eighth Army and Axis forces that resulted in a British victory that eliminated the axis threat in Egypt and sparked the beginning of the end of the western desert campaign.

By April 2006, Officer Cadet Wales had completed his officer training and was given his Commission as a Cornet, an antiquated way of referring to a second Lieutenant. He was assigned to the Household Calvary, part of the Household Division, which in part serves as the King's official bodyguard. Acting as royal security may seem a bit bland, but the Household Cavalry is much more than that. The Calvary is divided into the two most senior regiments of the British Army, so it was a great honor for Harry to be assigned to the Blues and Royals, otherwise known as the Royal Horse Guards and 1st dragoons.

This assignment was an active one, as well as a dangerous one. The Blues and Royals have served in Northern Ireland, Germany, and Cyprus. They saw action in the Falklands wars in 1982, in Bosnia in the mid-90s, and more recently in the wars in Iraq and Afghanistan. In fact, in 2006, it was announced that Harry's unit would be deployed to Iraq sometime in the following year. An uproar and public debate ensued regarding whether a prince should be allowed to fight on the front line. In the following chapter, we'll discuss the issues at hand, as well as how they affected Harry's future as a commissioned officer.

Chelsy Davy

On Harry's 21st birthday, he sat for an interview for The Guardian, a major London-based newspaper and online news source. While the article touched on various topics, including his father's relationship with Camilla Shand, the subject of Harry's love life came up. By this time, he'd already started a drama-filled, on again off again relationship with Chelsy Davey. in the interview, Harry said about his girlfriend, "I would love to tell everyone how amazing she is, but once I start talking about that, I have left myself open. There is truth, and there are lies, and unfortunately, I cannot get the truth across." Indeed, the public would often find it hard to get to the truth regarding Harry and Chelsy's relationship, as will touch on in the following chapter.

Chelsy Davy, one year Harry's younger, is the daughter of a Zimbabwean businessman named Charles Davy, a safari farmer who at one time was one of the largest landowners in Zimbabwe. Chelsy was sent to England to attend school where she met Harry. By 2005, at the time of Harry's above-mentioned interview, Chelsy was studying for a degree in economics at the University of Cape town in South Africa. However, she got her bachelor's degree in 2006 and returned to England to study law at the University of Leeds.

Chelsy would continue to be a part of Harry's life for many years. But more on that later.

CHAPTER 4

Afghanistan and Back

In eras past, a kind of Prince would join his men on the frontlines of battle, boosting the morale of his troops, coordinating battle strategies in real-time, and leading as an example of strength and bravery. Of course, the King would not be reckless, recognizing that his value on the battlefield was much more than how well he could swing a sword or act, and he would surround himself with his mightiest warriors as both a protection and a show of royal force. Then again, no ancient or medieval king had to worry about a single Hellfire missile or well-placed mortar taking his life and the lives of all those around him.

As soon as it was made public that Prince Harry's unit would be deployed in Iraq the following year, a public debate erupted regarding whether a member of the royal family should serve in such a dangerous place. On one side were figures within the Ministry of Defense who felt such a deployment would constitute an unnecessary risk and that Harry should be shielded from the front line. In a statement given in April of 2006, a spokeswoman for the MOD said that Harry's "overt presence might attract additional attention." In other words, because Harry would be such a high-profile target, his presence would put him and the men he commanded at greater risk.

On the other side of the argument were John Reid, the Secretary of Defense, and Harry himself. Reid Defended Harry's right as a commissioned officer to serve on the frontline, and the Prince publicly agreed with that sentiment. "If they said 'no, You can't go frontline,'" Harry said, then I wouldn't drag my sorry ass through Sandhurst, and I wouldn't be where I am now." It seemed likely that Harry would be allowed to fight after all since even the MOD had stated in their original statement that Harry should be able to "undertake the fullest range of deployments."

The months passed, and the debate raged on. At one point, Harry threatened to quit the army if he was kept behind in safety while the rest of his regiment went to war. Finally, the government announced in February 2007 that Harry would be sent to Iraq as part of the third mechanized division. Harry would be off to war in May or June of 2007.

A Last-Minute Reversal

As late as April 8, 2007, Harry's deployment was practically a sure thing. General Sir Richard Dannatt, the then head of the British Army, said he'd personally decided to allow Harry to serve as a troop commander in Iraq. Then, suddenly, all those plans fell apart.

It was May 16, and Harry's deployment was imminent. Suddenly, Dannatt announced that Harry would not be going to Iraq. By this point, several groups had made threats to his life, and it was decided that, with Harry being considered a high-value target, both he and his men would be in extreme danger if he went to Iraq.

Publicly, Harry expressed his disappointment. But, as we'll see next, he was not out of options yet.

Secret Deployment To Afghanistan

A key problem with Harry's first assignment was how public it was. His deployment was announced a full year ahead of time and debated on new sites throughout that time period. Any enemy of the UK, NATO, or western society could easily take advantage and start making devious plans. When Harry did finally make it to war, it was done out of the public eye.

In June 2007, Harry traveled to CFB Sheffield, a military base outside Medicine Hat, Alberta, Canada. It was announced that he would be training alongside members of the Canadian forces and British Army in preparation for a possible tour of duty in Afghanistan. Then, no other news came out about the Prince for the rest of the year. It wasn't until early the following year that the story of where Harry had been broke out. The German newspaper *Bild* first leaked the information, followed by the magazine *New Idea* out of Australia. At that point, the proverbial cat was out of the bag, and the British Army had no choice but to announce that Harry had already been secretly sent to Afghanistan and that news of his deployment had been locked down by virtue of a news blackout, which *Bild* and *New Idea* had stubbornly breached.

In February of 2008, the British Ministry of Defense confirmed what the leaks had already dug up: Harry had been in the Helmand Province of Afghanistan for the last ten weeks, since late 2007, serving as a Forward Air Controller, which is a soldier on the ground who provides eyes-on intel and guidance for close air support, mostly to make sure the aircraft hit the intended target with a minimum of collateral.

Harry had finally gotten what he wanted. While stationed in Helmand Province, which is in the southern part of Afghanistan and is the largest of the country's 34 provinces by area, the Prince had helped British troops made up of Nepalese Gurkha soldiers repel a Taliban attack. He'd also performed patrol duty in hostile areas as part of his job as a Forward Air Controller. He'd certainly been on the front line, and he was still both safe and handling the assignment as a pro.

Immediately, the public debate heated up again now that the news was out. Harry had to be pulled out of Afghanistan because the media was tripping over themselves to cover Harry's "war hero" story, and this would only put him, his comrades, and the journalists at extreme risk. However, Harry had shown the world that he could do his job as an officer. He'd also become the first member of the royal family to serve in an active war zone since his uncle, Prince Andrew. Andrew had flown helicopters during the Falklands War in Argentina in the 80s, and now, some 25 years later, Harry joined his uncle in the ranks of British Royal War Heroes.

In fact, Andrew's heritage would come to mean even more to Harry in the years ahead because the Prince's next move would be to join his uncle in becoming a helicopter pilot. This, as we'll see next, turned out to be the way for Harry to return to the battlefield—in an aircraft instead of on the ground.

Additional Training And Relationship

Things happened quickly for Harry after returning from Afghanistan. The media was abuzz with his exploits. In April 2008, he was promoted to the rank of lieutenant. The following month, his aunt, Princess Anne, the only daughter of Elizabeth II, presented Harry with an Afghan Medal, also called an Operational Service Medal for Afghanistan. The ceremony was held at the Combermere Barracks, a military installation just up the road from Windsor Castle.

Who else was present at that ceremony? Chelsy Davy.

Throughout 2008, media reports and online sources talked about the drama between Harry and Chelsy. They reportedly broke up and were together again on a regular basis. In January 2009, Chelsy announced via Facebook that their relationship was over. Yet other sources said they'd gotten back together again and didn't officially end things until sometime in early 2010. Either way, Chelsy Davy was definitely out of his life at some point after his first tour in Afghanistan and before he would ultimately return to the Middle East and active combat.

In October 2008, Harry attended the Defense Helicopter Flying School, a training facility based in Shropshire, England, which specializes in teaching aircrews with the Eurocopter Squirrel HT1 and Bell Griffin HT1. Harry's brother, Prince William, had already been to the school and was now a sub-lieutenant in the Royal Navy and the Royal Air Force. While Harry did eventually get to see action on the front line, William sadly knew he wouldn't since he was higher in the succession to the throne and would therefore be even more protected than his brother.

By May 2010, Harry was presented with his wings, also called a flying brevet, at a ceremony at Middle Wallop Army Air Corps Base, where Prince Charles gave the wings to his own son. By April 2011, Harry was promoted to Captain and had continued his training to the point of now having his Apache Flying Badge. He'd soon be cleared to return to the front line in Afghanistan, but now as an Apache helicopter pilot. All that remained was for him to do a short stint of additional training, which he completed in the US, specifically in California and Arizona. More on his time in California will be discussed in the following chapter.

CHAPTER 5

The Dark Years

In June 2011, when asked about his love life, Harry described himself as "100 percent single." Even though Chelsy Davy did attend the wedding of Prince William and Catherine Middleton in April of that year, she told the press that she and Harry would not marry because they had a basic incompatibility in what they wanted in life.

In 2011 Prince Harry was decidedly single and was completing his training as an Apache helicopter pilot. Those outward appearances could be deceiving, however. In Harry's case, his life was taking a downward turn emotionally, and the events of the next couple of years would only make things worse.

The Party Life

Arriving in California for his training in October of 2011, Harry soon made it to the top of his class. The Naval Air Facility, a top-notch base that handles training regimens for pilots of all kinds of aircraft, including the Blue Angels aerobatics flight demonstration squadron, a team of pilots famous throughout the united states by military and civilian flight enthusiasts alike, is located just outside of El Centro, California. El Centro has a population of under 50,000 people, meaning it doesn't provide much in the way of entertainment while trainees have downtime. That said, San Diego is nearby, and there is plenty to do there.

Harry was quickly spotted by tabloids and serious journalists alike at popular eateries and shops around San Diego. Newspapers across the US gave regular updates on his movements and the things he was up to around town. And what did the media especially grab onto? His love of parties. The news articles started to pour in.

Because of this, and because of the speculation in American newspapers like the *Washington Post* that the Prince would soon grow bored of San Diego and turn his attention to an even bigger party town nearby—Las Vegas—Harry was pulled from his training in the US and was transported back home to England, where he completed his Apache certifications at Wattisham Airfield in Suffolk.

Harry continued to embrace the party life, and this

quickly developed into self-destructive behavior. In February 2012, Queen Elizabeth II celebrated the so-called Diamond Jubilee, the 60-year anniversary of her ascension to the throne. This celebration was a big deal because no other monarch of England had managed 60 years on the throne since Queen Victoria. During that time, Harry suffered major anxiety and panic attacks. He would also suffer from burnout after working so hard as an officer and pilot.

"I wasn't drinking Monday to Friday," he would later say about this period in his life, "but I would probably drink a week's worth in one day on a Friday or a Saturday night."

Meanwhile, Harry was managing to hide this downward spiral fairly well. He continued to get good marks in his training, and he was now looking at possibly returning to Afghanistan as a helicopter pilot. He also got a new girlfriend. He started seeing Cressida Bonas, an English actress and model, in May 2012 after Princess Eugenie introduced them. On the inside, however, Harry was not doing well. And things were about to get even worse.

Return To Afghanistan

Harry arrived in Afghanistan for the second time on September 7, 2012. This should have been a good thing. After all, it's what Harry wanted, what he'd been training for all these years. And it would also serve as a distraction for him and an opportunity to regain some structure in his life. But things didn't quite work out that way.

He served as part of the 662 Squadron, 3 Regiment, Army Air-Corps, a group of over 100 highly-trained men and women. His assignment would be as the co-pilot and gunner on Apache helicopters. As the one that would pull the trigger on the aircraft, he'd later talk about the impact killing insurgents had on him. "We fire when we have to, take a life to save a life." He also compared flying the helicopters to playing on a PlayStation or Xbox.

But playing pilot and soldier wasn't all fun and game. As soon as Harry arrived in Afghanistan, the Taliban made plans to either kill or kidnap him. In an interview with Reuters, Taliban spokesman Zabiullah Mujahid said, "We are using all our strength to get rid of him, either by killing or kidnapping. We have informed our commanders in Helmand to do whatever they can to eliminate him." So Harry had a pretty large target on his back right away.

Within ten days of his arrival in the country, Harry had to be moved to a safer location because an attempt was made on his life.

The British government was more supportive of Harry's fighting on the front line this time around. While extra security precautions had to be taken, there were no plans to pull him out of the country. Defense Secretary Philip Hammond said that the Prince would face "the same risk as any other Apache pilot."

In January 2013, Harry completed his 20-week tour in Afghanistan and returned home, and in July of that same year, he was promoted to an Apache aircraft commander.

Still, the combat he saw and the lives people lost around him would take a toll on him. Thankfully, as we'll see in the following chapter, Harry did find a way to cope with all of this trauma. It would start with him helping others, and then he'd finally also take the time to seek out help for himself.

CHAPTER 6

Helping Others

Right after getting back from Afghanistan the second time, Harry started to take an interest in military veterans, especially those that had been injured while fighting wars abroad, both in the United States and the UK. All throughout 2013, images appeared in tabloids and newspapers, not of a partying Harry going to clubs or eateries, but a serious-faced veteran having frank discussions with fellow soldiers who were now missing a limb or were scared by combat in some other way.

In January 2014, the Ministry of Defense gave Harry a staff officer role, assigned to provide organization, planning, and support to fellow soldiers. His responsibilities included helping in the planning and execution of significant projects and big, commemorative events in and around London.

This non-combat role would allow Harry to spend more time thinking about how to help the wounded, which led to his next big project.

The Invictus Games

In March 2014, Harry launched Invictus Games, an international sporting event specifically for wounded, injured, and sick servicemen and women that were either veterans or still actively serving in the military. Harry chose the name of these Paralympic-style games carefully; the name *Invictus* means "unconquered," the perfect way to symbolize the fighting spirit of wounded warriors.

Harry would later write an article for *The Sunday Times* about his experiences in Afghanistan during those two tours. He experienced and saw things that would traumatize him for life, but he chose not to dwell on such things. Instead, he was inspired by the strength and bravery of his fellow soldiers, and he was moved to help those that didn't come back from the front line whole. After a trip to see the US's Warrior Games, which is essentially the same idea, Harry made it his mission to launch the Invictus Games in the UK.

When the games were soon to launch, Harry promoted them through interviews with media organizations like BBC Radio 2. In one such interview, he said that the games "is basically my full-time job at the moment, making sure that we pull this off."

In April 2014, Harry and Cressida Bonas ended their relationship, but they reported to the press that the split was "amicable" and free of the drama of Harry's previous breakup.

Early in 2015, Harry took on an even more focused role within the British military to support wounded service personnel, working with the Ministry of Defense's Personal Recovery Program. He worked alongside several veteran-focused and wounded-warrior-style charities to better organize any help he could give them.

It seemed that focusing on helping others in this way was giving Harry a much-needed focus in his life, a kind of therapy to help him work through his own problems.

Leaving The Military

In the spring of 2015, it was made public that Harry would be leaving the British Armed Forces later that year. While he considered his future, the same announcement said he'd continue to work with the MOD on a voluntary basis to continue to bring help to injured and sick veterans through the government-sponsored recovery programs.

Before finishing up his military career, however,

Prince Harry would spend four weeks in Australian army barracks, seconded to the Australian Defense Force. It's interesting to think that, once again, Harry would go to Australia in order to close off a chapter in his life. The first time was during his gap year, as he was done being a student and was ready to be a soldier.

Harry would later say that the ten years he spent in the military were the "Happiest times of my life."

He continued to support veterans and wounded soldiers in a variety of ways, as promised. In the fall of 2015, Harry toured several military bases in the US alongside Michelle Obama, and he continued to organize charities to support soldiers back in the UK.

Getting Help

In July of the following year, Harry started a relationship with a beautiful American actress, Meghan Markle. She would prove to be invaluable in helping Harry get through the issues that he'd kept with him most of his life.

Not long after they started dating, Harry worked alongside his brother and sister-in-law Catherine to launch the mental health awareness campaign called "Heads Together." In order to finally be convinced to seek the help he needed for himself, Harry had to make sure his brother, who'd faced all the same challenges growing up, got the help he needed, as well. His brother, in turn, gave Harry the support he needed.

Harry later opened up about finally going to counseling years later. He thanked his brother for helping him to finally take this step. "It's all about timing," Harry said. "And for me personally, my brother, you know, bless him, he was a huge support to me. He kept saying this is not right, this is not normal, you need to talk to [someone] about stuff, it's OK."

He also took up boxing as a way to work through his anxiety. Finally, after all these years, he was able to address his mother's death, the hardships of his youth, and even more recent tragic events he'd witnessed while on the front line.

Harry was ready to move on with his life, having left the past behind him. And the direction he wanted to go in involved the young woman already by his side. Harry was ready to start a family.

CHAPTER 7

A Family Man

Meghan grew up in California, the daughter of an Emmy Award-winning television writing director and director of photography. Meghan was used to the Hollywood television scene since she practically grew up on set, visiting her father after her parents divorced while she was very young.

Later in life, Meghan took an interest in theater and television herself, but breaking into the business proved difficult because, according to Meghan, her mixed-race heritage made it difficult for her to fit various roles. "I wasn't black enough for the black roles and I wasn't white enough for the white ones," she once commented to CNN. Eventually, she got work on a few series, but her big break was undoubtedly landing the role of Rachel Zane on the USA series *Suits*, a role she had from the summer of

2011 until late 2017. By the end of her acting career, she was making $50,000 per *Suits* episode.

Meghan was married to the film producer Trevor Engelson for a short time. They dated for years, but the actual marriage only lasted 18 months before they were separated. Then, in 2016, Meghan began dating Prince Harry. Her life was turned upside down after that point.

Many in the media and public loved Meghan and Harry's relationship, but there were also plenty of haters and trolls. In November 2016, Harry's communications secretary released a statement that expressed the Prince's personal concern about various negative and false statements made about Meghan on the internet and in the media.

Despite this negativity, their relationship continued to progress, and they started making public appearances together the following year.

Wedding Bells

In November 2017, Prince Charles announced Harry and Meghan's engagement, which prompted mostly positive comments from the media. Many were happy to see someone of mixed race potentially enter the royal family.

The wedding itself was a hugely anticipated event, like many royal weddings. The fact that Markle was an American celebrity on a hit TV show made the wedding an even bigger deal. They invited personal friends, favorite celebrities, and a few local government officials, as well as the royal family.

Meanwhile, Harry was busy in other ways. At the end of December 2017, he was named Captain General Royal Marines, a title given to the ceremonial head of the Royal Marines. Prince Philip, Harry's grandfather, had served in the role before Harry.

On May 19, 2018, the wedding was held at Windsor Castle, as was described in the introduction of this book. That same day, Harry was also given several important titles from his grandmother, Queen Elizabeth II, including Duke of Essex. He was also promoted to Lieutenant Commander of the Royal Navy, Major of the British Army, and Squadron Leader of the Royal Air Force.

The wedding ceremony was followed by a more intimate party of about 200 close friends and family.

Married Life

Harry and Meghan seemed to take to married life very well after the wedding. They initially lived at Nottingham Cottage in London, a lovely home on the ground of Kensington Palace, which has often been the temporary residence of various members of the royal family, or even staff, employees, or friends of the family.

It was soon discovered that Meghan was pregnant, and that prompted the couple to look for more suitable living quarters in the country. They moved to Frogmore Cottage, right next to Windsor Castle. Millions of pounds were paid to refurbish the cottage.

Finally, on May 6, 2019, Harry's first child, Archie Mountbatten-Windsor, was born. Harry was now a husband and a father. But family bliss wouldn't last, and the new family would soon grow restless in the UK.

CONCLUSION

The public had little idea of Harry and Meghan's difficulties within the royal family. But it soon became apparent that they would not be staying in the UK. In March 2020, their royal office cat Buckingham Palace was closed, and Harry announced that the couple would stop "undertaking official engagements in support of the Queen."

Soon after, they left to stay in the US and Canada for a while. That so-called temporary trip became permanent in June when they bought a house in Southern California, the former estate of Riven Rock in Montecito, California. Meanwhile, Harry had also stepped down from all his official military appointments.

In July, Meghan suffered a miscarriage. Through this time, they were basically separated from the royal family, giving up any responsibilities and ties they could.

In 2021, Oprah Winfrey sat down with both Harry and Meghan, and for the first time, they expressed their feelings about living in the UK with the royal family, saying they didn't feel comfortable.

Of course, a great deal of drama erupted from these comments, but both Harry and Meghan have since reiterated that they are simply happier in the states, where they've built a happy family life for themselves. They even have a chicken coop on their estate, where they take care of hens rescued from a factory farm.

Two more big things happened in 2021. First, Harry and Meghan had their second child, Lilibet Mountbatten-Windsor, and Harry produced a documentary about his life and experiences called *The Me You Can't See*. In the documentary, Harry opens up for the first time about those dark years discussed in this book.

In 2022, Harry and Meghan returned to the UK for a sad ceremony, the funeral of his grandmother Elizabeth. They were respectful and moved to tears during the funeral, and it was evident that, even though they may have developed personal differences with the queen and others of the royal family, they still loved them dearly.

Harry's story is about a sense of duty and responsibility. He felt a duty as a young prince, then as a soldier later in life. He passed through difficult times emotionally, but it was his sense of duty to his fellow soldiers that moved him to focus on helping others.

In the end, even his sense of duty moved him to separate from the royal family. In what way? Because now, as a husband, he had a duty to protect his own family and help them feel happy and safe.

Harry went to hell and back emotionally, but he pulled through, becoming a better father, leader, and person as a result. And what he chooses to do now with those qualities will undoubtedly inspire others to follow their own course and help others around them. What better legacy could one leave?

Made in United States
Orlando, FL
10 January 2023

28549236R00032